Lost In The Words Of Reality

Poems of Navigation

Juanita Jones

BookLeaf Publishing

India | USA | UK

Made with ❤ on the BookLeaf Publishing Platform
www.bookleafpub.in
www.bookleafpub.com

Dedication

This book is dedicated to all those who inspired the words within these pages and all the family and friends who've given me their time to read the first and final drafts of my pieces.
Hoping for many more decades of this with you.

Preface

We all share one planet and one human race yet we all have very distinct experiences. We build our villages as we grow upon our experiences and interactions then to shapes our perspectives. Finding ourselves and where we fit can be difficult, but if we are lucky we'll find and build a village as diverse as our emotions and experiences. A village that encompasses and welcomes everyone but holds tight those who we know will be there every day and time we need a hand up or a partner for support.

Each poem in this collection is an observation of the global society and the challenges faced as choices are made and sides are taken, but they are from a perspective this writer felt was necessary. Each poem interpreted a moment not the entire story and was meant to spark emotions, maybe even a conversation or two.

To find out more about the author she can be found at

WriterLostInWords.wordpress.com
instagram.com/Poet_tree70
@Poetree.bsky.social

Other books by the author:
A Glimpse of Today Poetry Pictures
Life In Motion

Acknowledgements

There are people who come into your life for a reason, even if you don't realize it at that moment. For me those people were great teachers and librarians who spurred my desire to escape with books that took me on many adventures. They will never realize their influence or how they saved my life so that I could become who I am today because they were selfless, giving months or a year to my lifetime hoping to make a small impact. Many of those teachers and librarians anchored me during moments of chaos without even knowing it, giving me the tools I would use throughout my life to build me. A lifetime of learning has provided me with so many teachers, good and bad, who went about their career never expecting a thank you at the end of our time together so I would like to extend a thank you to all the great teachers I had. Librarians, the most knowledgeable and amazing people I've ever encountered, are who cultivated my love of reading and writing through book recommendations. Those book recommendations were the start of my path of discovery and learning that let me find myself and my future which is why they deserve a thank you from me as well.

1. Is it at the door?

1,2,3,4
Is it at the door?
1,2,3,4
Is it at the door?
1,2,3,4
Is it at the door?

Boom!
War has come a knocking,
Down fall the walls
Of all,
Decimating past and future.

1,2,3,4
Is it at the door?
1,2,3,4
Is it at the door?
1,2,3,4
Is it at the door?

Blasting openings, then collapsing homes,
Two arms carrying a world,

As well as it's bones,
Only to discover what rubble buries
Isn't always dead.

1,2,3,4
Is it at the door?
1,2,3,4
Is it at the door?
1,2,3,4
Is it at the door?

Boundaries moving,
Shrinking until they are choking.
All those enclosed.
Leaving only bodies for bulldozers
To grind into the land.

1,2,3,4
Is it at the door?
1,2,3,4
Is it at the door?
1,2,3,4
Is it at the door?

Bound to the land.
Bound by oppression.
Both intertwined

As screens document
The erasing of all upon that land.

1,2,3,4
Is it at the door?
1,2,3,4
Is it at the door?
1,2,3,4
Is it at the door?

Let me get that.
The table is set.
The dishes are empty>
Please come
For our culture, we will not forget.

1,2,3,4
Is it at the door?
1,2,3,4
I'm seven.
1,2,3,4
I want to lay with all those I love.

War is at my door.
No matter if
I lock it shut,
Hold it open,

Or lie under it.

I don't want to be er

2. Half Your Heart

Half Your Heart

All I ask
Is for half of your heart.
For when we come together
We create a full heart.
I want a partner,
Who'll provide the encouragement
To push to strive onward,
Who will stand side by side
In times of fear and success,
Who will comfort
In moments of sadness,
Who will smile without knowing
Every time our eyes glimpse each other,
Who will embrace crazy adventures
When opportunities present,
Who will provide logic
When emotions push irrational decisions,
Who will laugh
Throughout difficult and good times.
For this is my promise to you,
Partner,
Together we'll be a whole,

Which is why
I'll only every ask
For half of your heart
In exchange for half of mine.
Partners.

3. A Storm

A Storm

Its wrath
Entered as a squall.
It's tempestuous nature
Touched all.
Lies of gale force raged
Roaring storms of fists
Flailed in anger,
Blooding many.
Bursting into lives,
Words of hate,
Ripping apart creations
With emotional destruction,
Blustering passion,
From hearts and minds,
Igniting cold raging fires
Of hate that froze all,
Replacing and filling
All space with an icy emptiness.
The storm of
Lies versus truth,
No end predicted
for the foreseeable future.

4. What You Hid

Eyes wide open,
Watching you find yourself,
Just wish it didn't take
Ten damn years of
That mask weighing on you
While living the expected life.
Ten damn years of
Reviving trust and love,
For your deception
To crush them to dust.

Both of us realizing
Oxygen was becoming scarce
When truth surfaced,
Without notice,
As one of the fragments
Of the relationship
And that betrayal
Pierced the hope
Cultivated over a decade.

Then the words came
Maybe you shouldn't come home
You've got something

To work through.
You've been doing it for sometime,
But now you need to do it alone.

Severed from each other,
Moving in two different directions,
Truth should be our destination,
But if that mask remains
One of us
Will never reach it.

5. Every Night

Dreams oscillating within the scape of sleep,
Pushing aside nightmares of reality,
Making them the curtains
Minds pull open
Revealing the alternative.
When sleep ends abruptly,
Minds whip the curtains close,
Exposing reality for all its grit and horror,
Which hearts and souls seek refuge from.
Within the darkness,
Moon's rays slice through
The shades of night,
As hands clench sheets and blankets.
Now minds race alongside replays of days,
Choices are second guessed,
Missed opportunities' regret punches guts,
Taking all the breath from lungs,
Leaving gasping shadows upon beds.
Some submit while others fight.
The rising sun will reveal the survivors,
And who will fight on.

6. What Lies Beneath

The sands greeted
Bare feet with every step.

Did the gritty grains take you back
To the beaches?
To those happy moments
Servicemen cherish?

The foamy water's edge
Embraced our ankles
As each crashing wave
Voiced its greeting.

Are you still here
Upon this shore?
Or are you beneath its mirrored surface?
Looking for the boys you lost?
The boys who didn't have the strength
To stay afloat for days?
Do you see your ship's metal skin?
Are the guns still attached?
Can you make out the wound that ripped it open?
Is there peace beneath the surface
For all the souls entombed within

That battleship's gray skin?

When you go beneath
Do you find your peace?
For I see your struggle
Upon the land you're now stranded,
For beneath your skin i
Is survivor's pain,
Breaking your heart as it shreds your spirit
For boys of war are brave
Until losses,
Shoved deep beneath the uniform
Rise up and crash into a memory.
I held your hand
As well as my tears and words
Hoping today would not be the day
You chose to live beneath with the past.

7. Preview

When summer provides a preview,
The yard gets a makeover
When the evening's darkness covers
A bit later,
The wind entices a moment of nature's music,
While old acquaintances emerge nightly,
Lights dance
With the breaths of the fire,
Tonight nature dominates the conversation
And uninterrupted we are lulled into peace.
Ever so fleeting,
But embraced for every second.
Its rhythm pulsing through bodies,
Time no longer relevant,
Body and naturing merging,
Almost there...
Shatter
All is lost
As roaring engines engulf the night,
Smothering all other auditory pleasures.
A preview of summer,
The desired and dreaded.

8. A Sunny Day

Grasping at liquid hoping to remain a float
-the summery breeze blows within a memory

Icy water embraces the entire body
-brilliant sun rays warm the skin upon the grass

Waves race to push the body under
-radiant happiness basked the body

Great skies create a haze of loneliness
-luminous smiles shared between friends

Arms flail finding the solid mass of floating dead
-clarion filled the air with notes of love

Voices silent as hopelessness engulfs
-our sunny day at the post war park

Exhaustion draining the fight from every limb
-Sleep washed the energy from a day of
exploration

Death swept in with a watery grasp

A sunny day
Now all is black

9. She Wanted to Feel Pretty

It's gold chained strap
Was bold against
White leather,
Hanging from her shoulders
As her hands held tight
The water bottles.

Within the crowd,
On the dust strewn street,
She struggled
To handle her items.
She'd stop,
Causing the crowd to part,
As she shifted her purse,
With its front flap,
shaped like an envelope
And
Edged with gold thread,
From her shoulder
To her hand.
Grasping its handle,
While the chain strap
fell towards her feet.

With small hands,
Gritty from the path's dust,
She grasped tightly
The bag's handles,
Recalling feeling pretty.
She recalled that past moment,
Embedded deep,
But she remembered
How pretty made her smile.

There aren't many memories
Of her brief 4 years
But pretty was one.
Filled with colors and life,
Family and hugs,
Contrasting her now,
Abundant of gray,
And destruction,
And death.

Genocide
Has no pretty,
No life,
No childhood,
No homes,
No cities,
Yet there,

With its unlatched flap
And dangling gold chain,
Was a dream of pretty
For a 4 year old child.

Then her hands,
One empty,
One clutching her bag,
Grabbed up
Her water bottles from amongst
The moving legs
Of fellow refuge seekers.

Revealing
The empty compartments,
The unlatched front flap,
Opened and closed,
When she ran to join
Her family remnants.
Handling her responsibilities
A small smile escaped
When she took in her purse.

She felt pretty,
She felt her past
From so long ago,
But she remembered

How pretty made her smile
There aren't many memories
Of her short 4 years
But pretty was one.

10. We Are Not

A great nation we are not.
A great race we are not.
Freedom,
Fought so hard for
It filled...built cemeteries,
Now beaten down with childish words
And the ink of many pens
by occupants
with labels for leaders.
Equality's existence
Moving to extinction,
Freedom's excavations
Halted with explosive bans,
Individuality's emersions
Barricaded behind closed doors,
Because history is forgotten...
Rewritten,
Ignored,
Manipulated.

A great nation we are not.
A great race we are not.

Centuries of festering hate

Now choke hope and progress,
Anger becomes a mob commodity
Traded by a controlling minority,
Spurring violence,
Taking heartbeats
And pulverizing then into dust.

A great nation we are not.
A great race we are not.

Centuries of ignorance
Now bleed out carrying away lost futures,
Oaths of care and to do no harm
Are discarded for imaginary leaders
And works of fiction
Rewritten too often to cater
To the ruling mass
While ignoring the living masses.

A great nation we are not.
A great race we are not.

Centuries of judgements to justify,
Now pierce minds, hearts and flesh
Create divisions to obscure truth and facts,
Forcing invasions into bedrooms,
Relationships, friendships, and families,

With destructive intentions,
But their words will always say otherwise.

A great nation we are not.
A great race we are not.

Centuries of human beings
Dredging animalistic traits to the surface,
With the sole intention of
Erasing humans
Their pain,
Their needs,
Their lives,
Their ancestors,
Their heritage,
Their progress,
For the purpose of raising a few
As priceless
Upon the blood and bones
Of those deemed worthless.

A great nation we are not.
A great race we are not.

Centuries of being told free will is for all
In one voice,
But in another

Condemning free will choices,
He chose him,
She chose to be he,
She chose Allah,
He chose Waheguru,
He chose him
And she chose her for their forevers,
But manipulation and misinformation
Cultivate hurt, bruises, and deaths.
Free will choices only acceptable
When they align with what is told.

A great nation we are not.
A great race we are not.

Centuries of resistance
Against the same wrongs,
For complacency is easier
Then education
Causing history's repetition.
The Elders would have taught
The history if they weren't
Separated from their village
Or
Targeted for eradication
Or
Erased from the past.

Centuries of repetition
Creates futures of repetition
For
A great nation we are not.
A great race we are not.

11. I'd Rather Stand With the Animals Than Civilization

The sadist carry their holy books
Defiling them with their every word
As silence wraps the voice
And the mind deciphers.

I'd rather stand with the animals than civilization.

Her hands held her heart
Her soul
Then she opened her hands,
released the air from her lung
And blew their ashes into the wind.
Crumpling to the rubble filled earth
Alone.

I'd rather stand with the animals than civilization.

Cradled in loving arms,
The toddler whose antics
Filled gigs of phone memory

While bringing joy to hearts,
One last hug,
One last touch,
But not one final look or kiss,
For this toddler's face
Was ripped away as violently as his final breath.

I'd rather stand with the animals than civilization.

Searching for the heartbeats,
Holding the hands breaking through the rubble,
Gathering the bits and pieces
Of friends and family
Taken too soon,
Childhood moments no one desires.

I'd rather stand with the animals than civilization.

I'd rather stand with the animals than civilization
For civilization watches
As those labeled animals commit selfless acts.

12. Decades in a Moment

The camera pans,
Across the flooding road,
To focus on a sweat shirt,
With bold white letters
Declaring one
A "Dreamer."
With a smile,
The wearer blows a kiss
Through the falling rain
While huddled between friends
Under two umbrellas.
It's a smile of warmth,
A moment of joy,
Then reality explodes,
With a 2000 pound missile,
Obliterating the landscape behind them
Along with childhoods
And their smiles.
The group pushes closer,
Trying to be brave men
Within their seven
And twelve year old bodies
That war has aged
Through fear and lost,

But only in childhoods' imagination
Do umbrellas stop bombs.
In reality,
Their wide eyes,
Eyes that witnessed carnage
No child should ever see,
A glimmer of hope
Escapes through a smile,
A laugh,
A moment of childhood.
It's as fleeting
As lives are In war.
And viewers are left
Questioning
Can a "Dreamer" survive
A genocide?

13. Greatest Victory

There were moments
Standing wasn't an option
When words battled pain
Then gods and followers
Who stole futures
Then foundations
Forcing it all to crumble
Upon eradicated lives of differences

I'll greet you at the gates of death,
Cross the abyss and nether world,
Walk within the fires of their hell,
Gather on the lands of ancestors,
Put my hand out
To be pulled into an embrace.
We'll smile
For the first time
Since that time,
And with a drink in hand,
Recount the greatest victory.

For even in death,
Robes of hypocrisy
Never blessed your sacrifice,

But the life it gave,
With every recovered fragment
Assembled together,
Not perfectly,
Because recovery
Is about putting
Shattered pieces together,
Would celebrate that sacrifice.

I'll greet you at the gates of death,
Cross the abyss and nether world,
Walk within the fires of their hell,
Gather on the lands of ancestors,
Put my hand out
To be pulled into an embrace.
We'll smile
For the first time
Since that time,
And with a drink in hand,
Recount the greatest victory.

A recovered life,
Teetering on shattered foundations
Of before
And destroyed childhoods,
Rebuilding what survived
Into what was supposed to be,

Not what they demanded
Or violently imposed,
Yet always justified,
Until diffidence in voices and acts
Retrieved fragile futures.

I'll greet you at the gates of death,
Cross the abyss and nether world,
Walk within the fires of their hell,
Gather on the lands of ancestors,
Put my hand out
To be pulled into an embrace.
We'll smile
For the first time
Since that time,
And with a drink in hand,
Recount the greatest victory.

Shouldering two worlds
Full of the spirits of the lost
Within battered vessels
Of skin, bones and blood
Salted with tears of pain
Famila embraces can't touch
For jagged edges
Are sharpest within fear,
Nothing will return the past,

Nor the present,
But standing will be a step
Towards a future of much mending
And foundational repairs.

I'll greet you at the gates of death,
Cross the abyss and nether world,
Walk within the fires of their hell,
Gather on the lands of ancestors,
Put my hand out
To be pulled into an embrace.
We'll smile
For the first time
Since that time,
And with a drink in hand,
Recount the greatest victory.

Not within the hatred of their heaven
Or the evil of their hell,
A hell they brought and cultivated
Upon the earth's surface
To torture generations of others,
But within the embrace of earth
And the ancestors interred
Whether by fate
Or humanity's inhumanity,
A village will prosper.

I'll greet you at the gates of death,
Cross the abyss and nether world,
Walk within the fires of their hell,
Gather on the lands of ancestors,
Put my hand out
To be pulled into an embrace.
We'll smile
For the first time
Since that time,
And with a drink in hand,
Recount the greatest victory,

Surviving,
Thriving,
Prospering.

13. Stomp Goes the Night

Stomp goes the night,
Blinding those who wish not to see.
Books of hate, intolerance, and injustice
Searing their way into what's labeled education
Hoping no leaders emerge just followers.

Stomp goes the night
Hiding those who wish not to be seen.
Words of terror, intolerance, and death
Searing their way into what was community
Hoping to vanquish all differences

Stomp goes the night
Covering those who wish not to hear.
Acts of greed, rapacity, and covetousness
Searing their way into what was society
Hoping to raze all freedoms.

Stomp goes the night
Pushing those who wish not to understand.
Maneuvers of deception, hypocrisy, and duplicity
Searing their way into what was family
Hoping to decimate every connection.

Stomp goes the night
Crushing those who wish not to think.
Facades of patriotism, bravery, and strength
Searing their way into what were individuals
Hoping to cultivate mindless complicity.

Stomp goes the night
Stomp goes the night
Stomp goes humanity
Stomp goes humanity

14. Humanity's Death Shroud

Put down the book
look at the human.
Blood flows the same,
No matter the God you name.
Tears flow for the pain.

When voices are contained
Under the rubble of bombs
And debris of hate
And when they are silenced
By overflowing vessels
Stifling desperation and anger
With blades or piercing bullets
Demands for equality,
For freedom will pierce
Every eye, ear, and heart
So deeply embedded
They will cling like a death shroud.

Collective anger,
Collective hate,
Weaved together
For genocide.

With bombs
Autographed by children,
Indoctrinated with hated,
Detonating the annihilation
Of other children and their families,
Burying them deep
Into the land of ancestors,
No longer acknowledged
As human beings.

Airstrikes and bullets intertwine
For a single objective,
A cruel society reset,
Erasing histories of ancestors
Alongside a culture.
Futures lay bound within
Death's white shrouds
To be interred
Just below the surface
Of the land of a prison,
From which people clawed
Out a society to resuscitate a culture.
Now in the state of obliteration
The remaining fragments
Pile high hiding
What was so hated
So detested

So unwanted.
Ethnic cleansing
Washes away all
Including humanity.

15. (In)Humanity's Page

Put down the book,
Look at the human.
Blood flows the same,
No matter the God you name.
Tears flow for the pain.

When voices are contained
Under the rubble of bombs
And debris of hate,
And when they are silenced
By overflowing vessels
Stifling desperation and anger
With blades or piercing bullets,
Demands for equality,
For freedom
Will pierce
Every eye, ear, and heart
So deeply embedded
They will cling like a death shroud.

Collective anger,
Collective hate,
Weaved together
For genocide

With bombs,
Autographed by children
Indoctrinated with hated,
Detonating the annihilations
Of other children and families,
Burying them deep
Into the land of ancestors,
No longer acknowledged
As human beings.

Airstrikes and bullets intertwine
For a single objective,
A cruel society reset.
Erasing histories of ancestors
Alongside a culture.
Futures lay bound within
Death's white shrouds
To be interred,
Just below the surface
Of the land of a prison,
From which people clawed
Out a society to resuscitate a culture.
Now in the state of obliteration
The remaining fragments,
Pile high hiding
What was so hated,
So detested,

So unwanted,
Ethnic cleansing
Washes away all,
Including humanity.

16. Make Me Uncomfortable

Make me uncomfortable,
Because that's how lessons
Are learned.

Bring me to the table,
Then tell me to stand in the corner,
Because how else will I feel
What you have felt for generations.

Make me uncomfortable,
Because that's how lessons
Are learned.

Allow your voice to stir fear,
Fear that holds tongues and fists,
Because words alone
Will never reach that deep inside
To veins, vessels, hearts, guts, brains.

Make me uncomfortable,
Because that's how lessons
Are learned.

Stand on degrees earned with threats,

Threats to take equality,
Because work, no matter how hard,
Doesn't count when it's stained
By prejudice, hate and discrimination.

Make me uncomfortable,
Because that's how lessons
Are learned.

Judge my skin when I walk in,
Then mock it without delving into who I am,
Because privilege has exemption & blindness,
Not afforded to those with pigment and
A wake up only happens with experience.

Make me uncomfortable,
Because that's how lessons
Are learned.

17. Part 1: Slide On Over Part 2: See the World From My Side

Part 1: Slide on Over

Hey kid,
Why don't you slide on over,
Sit on down
And tell me a story.

Your road 's been long
With fear and hate.
On the grounds of a school
War waged
Without any end,
Except maybe yours.

Hey kid,
Why don't you slide on over,
Sit on down
And tell me a story.

The blood had spilled,
Staining the books,

Bruising the soul
As much as the skin,
Eroding layers of self,
But you were still there.

Hey kid,
Why don't you slide on over,
Sit on down
And tell me a story.

Before you think end,
Stories need sharing.
A child must have a chance.
Let the dreams out,
Then take them
To live without pain.

Hey kid,
Why don't you slide on over,
Sit on down
And tell me a story
Promising you will be here.

Part 2: See the World From My Side

Step on down,
See the world from my side.

The memories we share,
The nightmares you will leave me.
Take a look
Where I'm standing,
Picturing a world with me alone.

Step on down,
See the world from my side.

See the empty hand reaching,
Searching eyes waiting,
Silence filling our space,
See me where it was us
Living in a world alone.

Step on down,
See the world from my side.

Come let me in,
Your world is a piece of mine.
The darkness may engulf,
But a grasping hand
Can lead you from its isolation.

Step on down,
See the world from my side.

Open my eyes to your pain,
Share the burden
upon my shoulders,
It will seem bearable
For together is power over alone.

Step on down,
See the world from my side.

Let me into your world,
For our world is you and me
Revealed over time and acts,
But lurking is what's hidden
Embraced alone by fear.

Step on down,
See the world from my side.

Friend siblings bringing security
Against the world outside ours,
But collapses without one
For alone, either crumbles
Crushed into the earth never regarded,

Step on down,
See the world from my side

Where I will always be
No matter the secret,
No matter the darkness,
No matter the pain,
For we are more than friends

Step on down,
See the world from my side

Where I will shed my tears
Pound my fist into unforgiving earth
Scream for your return
For no one could replace you
Or the shattered shards of us

Step on down,
See the world from my side

Before I am force to decipher your side
From the outside of your coffin,
Above your freshly dug grave,
Alone and confused
Because you were afraid to let me into your side.

Step on down,
See the world from my side

Then let me help you
Keep your side from collapsing
And crushing you,
For our world depends on the other's
Alone's destruction is never confined

18. I Couldn't Because I was a Girl

I wanted to stand on the edge,
You said I couldn't because I was a girl,
So I jumped.
Seeing the beauty of the world,
Soaring miles above
Deploying my chute at the last inch,
Capturing the view once banned.

I wanted to run,
You said I couldn't because I was a girl,
So I sat behind the engine.
Open throttle,
Racing across the horizon,
Cutting through the clouds,
Cruising an atmosphere free of barriers.

I wanted to read,
You said I couldn't because I was a girl,
So I wrote
Ink filled pages,
Words forming speeches, books then lectures,
Smothering illiteracy,
Rewriting a resilient future.

I wanted to love,
You said I couldn't because I was a girl,
So I ran into unchosen arms.
Embracing gentle words and hands,
Demanding independence for each,
Resisting the archaic past's sexism,
Empowering strength through love.

I wanted to dance,
You said I couldn't because I was a girl,
So I created
Melodies and rhythms,
Vibrating from within the soul to the feet,
Freeing the ancestral spirit of music's movement,
Escaping society's bindings.

I wanted to be free,
You said I couldn't because I was a girl,
So I ran from home.
Walking the beach, streets and mountains,
Proving independence builds strength,
Uncovering an individual, me,
Finding alone without loneliness.

19. A Screen Away

I saw you on the screen.
I yelled be safe when the bombs exploded.
I watched as you raced to rescue the buried.
I held my breath as the snipers surrounded you.
I watched you fall.
I yelled for you to play dead.
I was a screen away.

I was a screen away.
My hands could only touch my keyboards,
But bombs are not controlled by my touch screens,
Blood can't be stopped with a key stroke,
Bodies can't be recovered from the rubble with a mouse.
I was a screen away.

I remember the lessons from history class,
The questions of how and why.
Now those answers
Play out in real time on screens.
Victims demonstrates
How easy genocide happens
While witnessed by a global society.
I was a screen away.

I was a screen away
But the side of right was clear,
Yet not for all.
I was a screen away,
Humanity was visible
But it was being pushed
Deep into the land
Of decimation,
Previously known as ancestral.
I was a screen away,
But others were there.

20. Rise

The words were to include all
Instead the choice exclude all but one
Then words wielded as weapons
Chained those stolen to the land,
Bonded partners to servitude,
Condemned every other to violence
Of words and fists.

With all,
But the one,
As less than whole,
Resistance brewed deep inside
The veins and vessels,
Carried from
The feet that let them stand,
To the hips that carried the next generations,
To the hearts that inspired desire and love,
To the mouths that announced the wrongs,
To the minds that delved into preconceived thoughts.

Resistance grew one body at a time,
Whether standing or six feet down,
Names are invoked,
To honor and remember.

The fight hasn't ended,
After centuries,
So upon bodies and shoulders
We resist the past mentality
Of privilege and separation,
For equality and freedom
Suffer the greatest losses
As privilege huddled by fires
And brimful tables
Where no seats invite newcomers.

Uninvited,
Unwelcomed,
Resistance stands
With chairs ready
To insert at the table
Of freedom and equality.
Whether the old table must be
Decimated for the new one to be erected,
Even if it is erected
On the bodies of privilege,
It will be where all are seated
One day.